Life Cycles

Mealworms

by Donna Schaffer

Consultant:
Richard Mankin, Ph.D.
USDA—Agricultural Research Service
Center for Medical, Agricultural,
and Veterinary Entomology

Bridgestone Books
an imprint of Capstone Press
Mankato, Minnesota

Bridgestone Books are published by Capstone Press
818 North Willow Street, Mankato, Minnesota 56001
http://www.capstone-press.com

Library of Congress Cataloging-in-Publication Data
Schaffer, Donna.
    Mealworms/by Donna Schaffer.
    p. cm.—(Life cycles)
    Includes bibliographical references (p. 23) and index.
    Summary: Describes the physical characteristics, habits, and stages of development
of mealworms.
    ISBN 0-7368-0209-6
    1. Meal worms—Life cycles—Juvenile literature. [1. Meal worms.] I. Title. II. Series:
Schaffer, Donna. Life cycles.
QL596.T2S36   1999
595.76'9—dc21

                                                                    98-53031
                                                                         CIP
                                                                          AC

Editorial Credits

Christy Steele, editor; Steve Weil/Tandem Design, cover designer; Linda Clavel,
    illustrator; Kimberly Danger, photo researcher

Photo Credits

Connie Toops, 20
David Liebman, cover, 4
James P. Rowan, 8, 14
Rob Curtis, 6, 10
Susan Fay, 12, 16, 18 (top and bottom)

Table of Contents

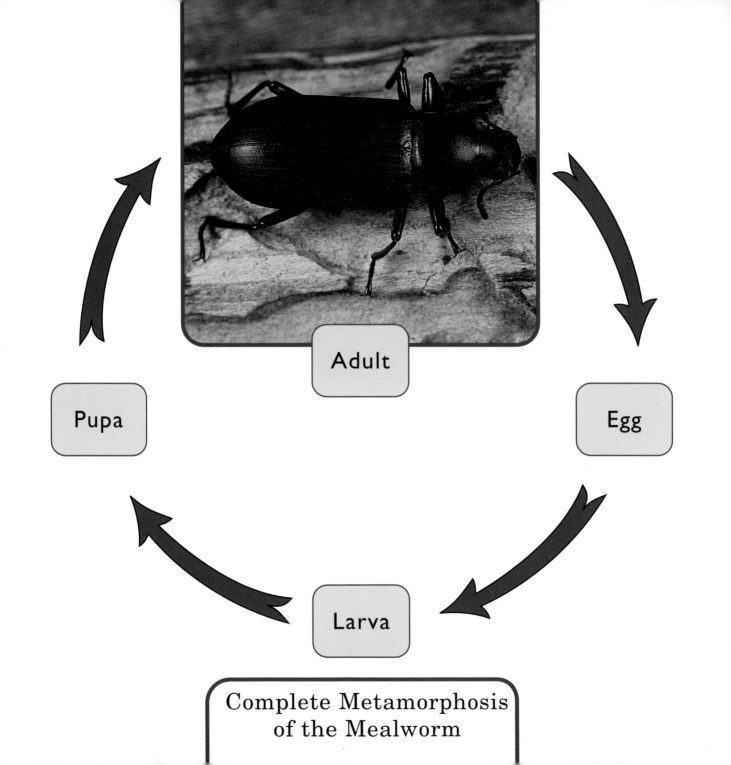

Adult

Egg

Pupa

Larva

Complete Metamorphosis
of the Mealworm

Life Cycle of the Mealworm

Mealworms go through complete metamorphosis. A mealworm's body changes form four times during complete metamorphosis.

Mealworms grow in eggs during the first stage of complete metamorphosis. Mealworms enter the second life stage after they hatch. During the second stage, mealworms are called larvas. Larvas become pupas during the third stage. During the pupal stage, the mealworm develops and grows adult body parts. Finally, the pupa becomes an adult mealworm.

These stages make up a mealworm's life cycle. Almost all living things go through this cycle of birth, growth, reproduction, and death.

Beetles

Mealworms are beetles. Beetles make up one-fourth of the animal world. Nearly 300,000 beetle species exist. Each species is a group with its own features. Mealworms are part of the darkling beetle family. Darkling beetles are active only at night.

Mealworms and other beetles are insects. Insects have three main body sections. These sections are the head, thorax, and abdomen. Eyes and antennas are on the head. Wings are attached to the thorax. The stomach is in the abdomen. Mealworms also have six jointed legs.

Beetles do not have bones. A hard exoskeleton covers the outside of beetles' bodies. Exoskeletons protect their soft bodies.

● ● ● ● ● **Beetles have two hard wings that cover two delicate flight wings. Adult beetles have a line down their back where the hard wings meet.**

About Mealworms

The first part of the name mealworm describes what these beetles eat. Meal is grain that has been ground into tiny pieces. The word worm describes the beetle's appearance at the larval stage.

The two kinds of mealworms are yellow mealworms and dark mealworms. They look slightly different. Yellow mealworms are lighter than dark mealworms. But both beetles share many features and habits.

Mealworms are scavengers. They eat whatever food they can find. They eat mostly grain and grain products such as corn, wheat, and flour.

Mealworms live in barns or places where people store meal. Mealworms usually live in the corners of barns or in other dark places.

Some people raise mealworms to feed pet birds, fish, and reptiles. Others buy mealworm larvas in pet stores to feed their pets.

● ● ● ● **People often call yellow mealworm larvas golden grubs. Many people use yellow mealworms as bait to catch fish.**

Mating and Eggs

Adult mealworms mate in the spring. The male climbs on the female's back. After mating, females lay eggs during a period of 22 to 100 days. Each female lays about 275 eggs on a food source such as meal.

Eggs are small and white. A sticky liquid covers the eggs. Powder from meal sticks to the liquid. The powder camouflages the eggs. The eggs blend in with their surroundings. Camouflaged eggs are hard for predators to find and eat.

Mealworms grow inside eggs for about two weeks before they hatch. Newborn mealworms eat meal right after they hatch. They will not need to search for food. The newborn larvas have begun the second stage of their life cycle.

● ● ● ● ● **Adult mealworms mate in the spring.**

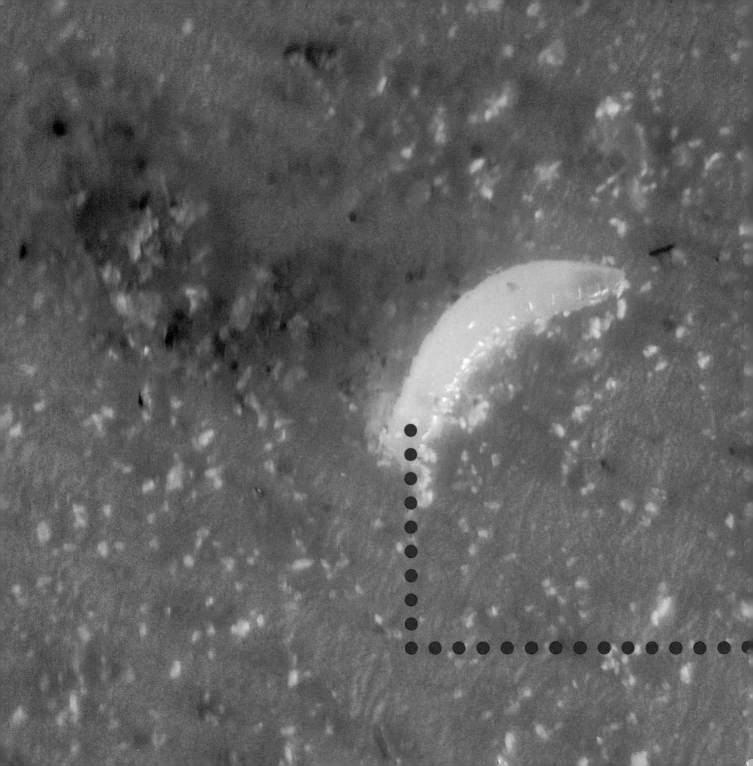

The Larva's Life

Newborn larvas are difficult to see. These wormlike creatures are white and very small. Larvas darken as they age.

Larvas do not have lungs. They breathe through tiny holes called spiracles. Spiracles are on the sides of the mealworm's body.

The larval stage is the longest stage of a mealworm's life cycle. Most mealworms stay in the larval stage for 30 to 90 days in warm weather.

Mealworms grow more slowly in cold conditions. Mealworms in cold areas can lie dormant in the larval stage. Their bodies rest until warm conditions return. Mealworms can stay dormant for up to two years when it is cold.

● ● ● ● ● **Young larvas eat the meal that surrounds them. In warm conditions, larvas will eat and grow for about three months.**

The Larva's Appearance

Thirteen segments make up the larva's body. The first segment is the head. The antennas, eyes, and mouth are on the head. Mealworms have three-part jaws that help them break food into pieces.

The next three segments make up the larva's thorax. Each segment on the thorax has a pair of legs. Legs help the mealworm move around.

The last nine segments form the mealworm's abdomen. The abdomen contains important organs. These body parts help the mealworm break down food, breathe, and mate. Adult females have organs that help them lay eggs.

Some organs help the larva recycle water from its food. Mealworms can live without water for many days.

This is a yellow mealworm larva. A shiny exoskeleton covers the mealworm larva's body.

Molting

A mealworm larva eats and grows. But the exoskeleton does not grow with the larva. The larva must shed its exoskeleton to grow. This process is called molting. A larva molts up to five times during its larval stage.

During each molt, a larva's exoskeleton splits. A softer and larger larva crawls out of the old exoskeleton. A larva eats and grows after each molt. Its exoskeleton becomes tight and hard. The larva is then ready to molt again.

A mealworm larva becomes thicker and longer after each molt. A fully grown larva is .8 inch (2 centimeters) thick. It is about 1.25 inches (3 centimeters) long.

Mealworm larvas usually hide when they molt. Molting larvas are easily caught by predators such as birds and frogs.

Pupas

After its last larval molt, the mealworm larva becomes a pupa. During this stage, a protective shell develops. At first, the pupal shell is white. The shell grows darker and hardens as the pupa grows.

The pupa does not eat or move. But many changes take place inside its shell. The larva's stubby legs grow into the jointed legs of an adult. Wings form. Eyes and antennas develop more fully. The body no longer looks wormlike.

The pupal stage lasts from 10 to 20 days. A pupa's hard shell splits when the adult mealworm has fully formed. The mealworm has molted for the last time. The mealworm is an adult. It has entered its final life stage.

● ● ● ● ● **The top photo shows how the pupa grows and changes. In the bottom photo, the adult is crawling out of its pupal shell.**

Adult Mealworm Beetles

Adult mealworms crawl out of their pupal shells. They usually reach this final life stage in summer.

At first, adults are white. Next, they become red-brown. Yellow mealworms then turn a shiny dark brown or black. Dark mealworms become dull black.

Adult mealworms are active at night. They may travel more than one-half mile (.8 kilometer) to search for food.

Adult mealworms live for five to 10 days. During this time, many mealworms will mate. Female mealworms will lay eggs, and the life cycle will begin again.

● ● ● ● ● **Adult mealworms often live near food sources such as corn.**

Hands On: Light Experiment

During the day, mealworms hide in dark places. During the night, mealworms are active and are attracted to light. Ask an adult to help you do this experiment to see how light attracts mealworms.

What You Need
Scissors

Two empty cardboard tubes

Clear plastic wrap

Black construction paper

One large box

Adult mealworms

One flashlight

Tape

What You Do
1. Cut a small hole in the large box.
2. Loosely tape plastic wrap to the top of one end of a cardboard tube. Loosely tape black paper to the top of one end of the other tube. Mealworms must be able to crawl underneath the material.
3. Place several adult mealworms in the open end of each cardboard tube.
4. Place the cardboard tubes inside the large box. The ends with the material should face the small hole.
5. Shine the flashlight through the small hole in the box. What happens?

The mealworms in the tube with the transparent material will crawl to the light. The other mealworms cannot see the light. They stay inside their tube.

Words to Know

antennas (an-TEN-uhs)—feelers on the heads of insects

camouflage (KAM-uh-flahzh)—coloring or covering that makes animals look like their surroundings

dormant (DOR-muhnt)—a state of rest

exoskeleton (eks-oh-SKEL-uh-tuhn)—a hard covering on the outside of an animal

metamorphosis (met-uh-MOR-fuh-siss)—the physical changes some animals go through as they develop from eggs to adults

molt (MOHLT)—to shed an outer covering so that a new one can grow

organ (OR-guhn)—a part of the body that performs a function

Read More

Greenaway, Theresa. *Beetles.* Minipets. Austin, Texas: Raintree Steck-Vaughn, 1999.

Mason, Adrienne. *Mealworms: Raise Them, Watch Them, See Them Change.* Buffalo, N.Y.: Kids Can Press, 1998.

Useful Addresses

Department of Entomology
Royal Ontario Museum
Toronto, ON M5S 2C6
Canada

Young Entomologists'
   Society
6907 West Grand River
   Avenue
Lansing, MI 48906

Internet Sites

Keeping and Raising Mealworms
http://www.icomm.ca/~dragon/mealworm.htm
Mealworms
http://seedsnet.stark.k12.oh.us/SEEDSKits/
   treasurehunt/mealworms.html
Yellow and Dark Mealworms
http://www.ag.ohio-state.edu/~ohioline/
   hyg-fact/2000/2093.html

Index